BSA A50/A65 TWINS

ALL MODELS
1962 - 1972

Roy Bacon

First published in the United Kingdom by:
Niton Publishing
PO Box 3. Ventnor. Isle of Wight PO38 2AS

Acknowledgements
The author would like to thank those who
helped this book by supplying the photo-
graphs. Most came from the EMAP archives
or *Motor Cycle News* by courtesy of the
editor, Malcolm Gough. Others came from the
Mick Woollet archive and somefrom the
author's files.

This edition published 1995 by
The Promotional Reprint Company Ltd,
exclusively for Selecta Book Limited.
Roundway, Devizes, Wiltshire SN10 2HR
and Reed Editions in Australia.

ISBN 1 85648 309 6

Printed in Hong Kong

Mike Hailwood with the BSA twin he used to win the production race at Silverstone in 1965; bearded Paddy Driver to left.

Contents

Introduction

The unit-construction BSA twins took over from the A7 and A10 series by having their basic mechanical design clothed in new castings. The opportunity was taken to revise some details, and the new models, in two capacities, were re-styled to change their lines, but the results were somewhat corpulent.

In time, this aspect was reduced with the arrival of more sporting models, especially those for the American market. These greatly extended the range for a year or two, but then it was consolidated into touring, sports and off-road machines. Later still, the job of the super-sports Spitfire was taken over by the Rocket 3 triple, and the range was given a final revamp for 1971.

By then, the company was in deep water financially so the end came soon. Behind, however, was left a legacy of good basic twins that found further favour in the classic bike revival of the 1980s. By then, solutions to their technical problems were known, tested and available, so the models became some of the more popular restoration projects

The first Spitfire road model, the MkII, on show in its 1966 form for the USA, with small tank and raised handlebars.

The A50 and A65

The new BSA twins were announced to the public, as the A50 Star and A65 Star, at the beginning of January 1962. They shared many components and were built to take over the role of the touring A7 and A10 models, which had formed the basis of the BSA twin line during the 1950s. The old models, in touring and sports forms, did stay in the lists for a year or two, but then were completely replaced by the new machines.

The new engines copied the old in the sense of being 360 degree vertical twins with overhead valves, a rear camshaft with gear drive, dry-sump lubrication and a four-speed gearbox. In other respects, they were new with revised details and a complete change to the electrics, which became alternator powered.

Both engines had a 74 mm stroke, which combined with a 65.5 mm bore to give the 499 cc capacity of the A50. For the A65, the bore was increased to 75 mm and the resulting capacity was 654 cc. The com-

First of the unit twins were the two Star models and this is the A65 version for 1962 with cable rear brake.

A 1962 A50 Star fitted out with legshields and windscreen from the list of options that were available.

pression ratio was quoted as 7.25:1 for both engines, but some BSA literature made reference to 7.5:1.

The bottom-half assembly was common to both engine sizes, with the exception of the gearbox sprocket and a timing cover badge. It was based on a cast light-alloy crankcase, which was split vertically on the centre-line of the engine. This joint line was continued in the top surface behind the cylinders, but below it, the right-hand casting was extended out to the left to enclose the gearbox.

The right-hand crankcase casting included the rear engine mounting lug and part of both front and bottom lugs. It was machined on its right-hand side to accept an inner timing cover, and it was recessed to accommodate the timing gears and a gearbox end cover in two separate areas with a cast wall between them.

The left-hand crankcase casting was simpler, but it included the inner wall of the primary chaincase. This had a large hole in it to give access to the gearbox sprocket and filled by a round plate carrying an oil seal

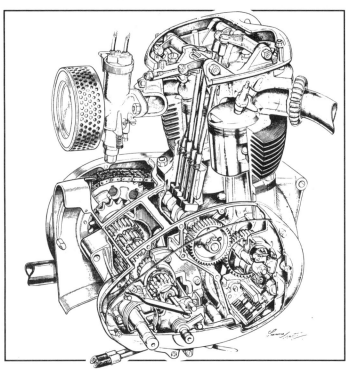

Line drawing of the unit construction twin engine, showing how the interior owed its layout to the earlier pre-unit motor.

that ran on the gearbox mainshaft. The area above the sprocket was cast over to enclose the rear drive chain.

Both crankcase halves had openings in their undersides to form a sump for the lubricating oil, which drained down after doing its work. The sump plate incorporated a mesh filter, and the area beneath the filter was connected to the scavenge pump by a short pipe.

Within the crankcase, the crankshaft turned in a ball race on the drive-side and a flanged bush on the timing-side. The bush also served as the oil feed into the crankshaft, and an undersize replacement was available to deal with wear. An oil

seal was fitted outboard of the ball race to separate the crankcase from the chaincase.

The crankshaft was a one-piece forging with a central flywheel pressed into place and retained by three radial bolts. A sludge trap was fitted within the crankpins, which were drilled for lubrication, and the crankshaft end-float was controlled by shims.

Light-alloy, forged connecting rods with shell big-end bearings and bushed small-ends were used. Each rod cap was held by two fitted bolts, which gave the location between the two parts, while the gudgeon pins were fully floating and retained by circlips. Each piston had a solid

The 1962 A50 Star was externally as the A65, except in the matter of its smaller front brake, with many common details on the inside.

skirt, three rings - including the scraper - and small valve cutaways.

The cylinder block was a one-piece iron casting, much as in the past, and was held to the crankcase by eight studs with nuts. A pushrod tunnel was cast into the rear of the block, and holes at the base of this accommodated the tappets, which were retained by circlips. Above the tappets went light-alloy pushrods with hardened steel ends,

This is the A65R sports Rocket which appeared for 1964 and is here out on a road test.

and these differed between inlet and exhaust, and again between the A50 and the A65.

The one-piece cylinder head was a light-alloy casting held to the block by a total of nine fixings, and a gasket was used to seal the joint. The valve sizes differed between the two engines, but otherwise the heads were common. Each casting had the rocker spindle supports and rocker box floor included, so only a simple cover was needed to fully

manifolds were bolted for the two engine capacities. The manifolds, in turn, carried either a single Type 376 Amal Monobloc carburettor with a 1 in. bore for the A50, or a Type 389 of 1-1/8 in. bore for the A65. On the exhaust side, the ports were bored for the pipes to be pushed in, while their finned clamps were decorative and played no part in holding the pipes in place.

The four valves were housed effectively within a single well, and

The standard A65, as built for 1964, with little change from its launch, other than to a rod operated rear brake.

enclose the valve gear. This made assembly much easier compared with the older design, which had a separate, one-piece rocker box and required a special tool to ensure that all the pushrods matched up with their rockers.

The new head casting had twin inlet ports to which alternative

each moved in a guide that was pressed in to a shoulder. Each was controlled by duplex coil springs seated in a cup that was located on the guide and retained by a collar and split collets.

There were six rocker spindle lugs, so each forged rocker was well supported. Each spindle ran across

For the USA in 1964 there was this A50CC(US) Cyclone Competition model built in scrambles form with open exhausts.

to carry two rockers and an assortment of spring and hardened washers to deal with end-float and wear. The inner rocker arms were fitted with hardened ball ends to match the pushrod cups, while the outers carried adjustment screws and locknuts to set the valve gaps.

The valves were opened by a camshaft positioned high up in the crankcase to the rear of the crankshaft. It was gear driven, a pinion on the right-hand end of the crankshaft being meshed with an intermediate

Alongside the Cyclone was offered the larger A65S/H Spitfire Hornet with more capacity, power and need for muscle to control it.

Single-carburettor Thunderbolt A65T/R only offered in this form for the USA in 1964.

gear, which it drove at half engine speed. In turn, this gear was meshed with the camshaft gear. The left-hand end of the camshaft drove a timed disc crankcase breather.

The intermediate gear had a further function, as it drove the auto-advance mechanism and cam for the coil ignition system. The two sets of points were mounted on a common plate (so could not be timed separately), and this was fixed to the inner timing cover. An outer cover enclosed the parts and had a small round access cover set in it to allow the points gap to be set. The cover carried a star badge to indicate the model.

Most American customers preferred this Lightning A65L/R with twin carburettors which was listed for 1965 as well as 1964.

The duplex-gear oil pump was fitted to the right-hand crankcase beneath the timing gears, and it was driven by a worm that was screwed on to the extreme right-hand end of the crankshaft. An anti-drain ball valve went behind the pump to make sure the contents of the oil tank did not migrate into the sump if the engine was not run for any length of time.

camshaft, tappets and timing gears.

The scavenge pump took the oil that drained back to the sump and returned it to the oil tank. A connection was taken from the return pipe, close to the oil tank, to feed the rockers, and this supply was fed into the rear of the cylinder head. Internal drillings took it to the spindles, and after lubricating the rockers, the oil drained down via the pushrod tun-

Home market A65 Star hitched to a sidecar for a 1965 magazine road test, which showed the twin well able to cope with the extra loads.

The feed pump sent the oil past a pressure release valve, set in the crankcase beneath the timing cover, and on to the timing-side main bearing. This took some oil for itself and directed the rest into the crankshaft to lubricate the big-ends. The oil was then thrown off to splash lubricate the cylinders and pistons, some falling into wells to deal with the

nel and holes drilled in the front of the head and block.

Engine power was transmitted to the clutch and gearbox by a triplex primary chain that was kept in correct tension by a curved slipper blade. This was set from below, but the design included a spring so that the blade could move to respond to chain variations as it ran round the sprockets.

The engine sprocket was splined to the crankshaft, and a Lucas RM19 alternator was mounted outboard of it to provide the electrical power. The drive was taken to a multi-plate clutch with a shock-absorber built into its centre, and this had a four-vane centre spider that was splined to the clutch hub, which was fixed to the gearbox mainshaft.

The clutch hub formed the inner

springs and raised by a simple lever attached to the inner timing cover. This moved a pushrod within the gearbox mainshaft, which acted against an adjuster screw in the centre of the pressure plate.

The whole of the primary drive was enclosed by a single, light-alloy cover held in place by a row of screws. It had two plugs set in its side, one being on the centre-line of the gearbox mainshaft and the other

The Cyclone Road model A50C(US) sold in America for 1965, but not as popular as the larger twins.

race for the loose rollers on which ran the cast-iron clutch drum. This had an integral triplex sprocket. The drum drove the plates that had the friction pads bonded to them, while the plain plates were splined to the centre hub which incorporated the shock-absorber. The plates were clamped by four compression

just ahead of it. One allowed the screw in the clutch pressure plate to be adjusted, and the other gave access to each clutch spring nut in turn. The two plugs were concealed by a small oval cover.

The four-speed gearbox was of conventional British design, with the output sprocket inboard of the

The home market Lightning A65L for 1965 when its twin carburettors and ample performance made it a popular choice for riders.

Both the Cyclone and Lightning for 1965 had similar sporting lines and smaller side covers to clear the air filters.

clutch and fitted to a sleeve gear, which was concentric with the main-shaft. There were ball races for the sleeve gear and mainshaft, while the layshaft beneath them ran in needle races. The gears were selected by two forks that moved on a single rod under the control of a flat camplate of quadrant shape. This plate was indexed from gear to gear by a simple positive-stop mechanism that went between the timing covers and ter-minated in a pedal on the right. The gearbox was separately lubricated

The Cyclone and Lightning in Clubman form were built for production racing and could select useful items from a long option list.

Special Lightning fitted with anti-car missiles for the James Bond film, *Thunderball*.

from the engine, so it had its own filler in the top of the crankcase. A standpipe set the level and also acted as the drain plug.

The right-hand ends of the gearbox shafts were supported by a plate that was fitted to the right-hand crankcase casting to form an end cover. The inner timing cover ran back for the length of the crankcase to enclose all this area, and the outer matched it. The inner cover had the speedometer drive shaft fitted to it and driven by a gear pinned to the right-hand end of the layshaft. A bush provided a housing for the drive shaft and a connection for the speedometer cable, which swept forward

from under the timing chest.

The kickstart mechanism, except for its return spring, went inside the inner cover. It comprised a quadrant gear that meshed with a pinion mounted on the right-hand end of the gearbox mainshaft and which drove it through a face ratchet. The kickstart pedal went on the right and did not fold.

The engine and gearbox assembly formed one unit that was bolted straight into the frame with just two small mounting plates at the rear. The frame was much as that used for the earlier twins with pivoted-fork rear suspension, so it was an all-welded tubular structure. It had

For 1966, the smallest road model became the A50R Royal Star, lost its nacelle and gained a more sporting line.

a single top tube, but duplex down-tubes that ran under the engine unit and up to join the top tube under the seat nose.

A rear subframe was welded on to support the dualseat and the tops of the rear spring units, which were hydraulically damped. The rear fork was welded and pivoted on Silent-bloc bushes pressed into its cross-tube. The spindle ran across between frame gussets welded to the seat tubes, so the rear fork was well supported. A centre stand was provided, while a prop stand was available as an extra.

Telescopic front forks, much as used by BSA for some years, were fitted and turned in cup-and-cone head races. They had external springs that were shrouded by extensions from the nacelle base pressing, which was capped by a small cover to conceal the fork top nuts,

The Thunderbolt matched the A50R in looks and style for 1966 when it was listed as the A65T.

steering head nut and handlebar clamps. The forks were hydraulically damped, and both solo and sidecar springs were listed in time. A steering damper was provided, with the friction discs below the headstock and their control knob above the top yoke.

Both wheels had similar hubs of composite construction, a cast-iron drum being riveted to an assembly of steel pressings that were brazed together. The drum design allowed

the shoes were fully floating so that they could take up their best position within the drum. The rear brake was of 7 in. diameter for both models, but at the front the A50 repeated the 7 in. size, while the A65 had an 8 in. anchor. In either case, the front backplate was located to a fork lug, but the back had a torque stay.

Rear brake operation was by one of two systems, and in either case the left-side brake pedal was mounted on a cross-shaft that ran

The 1966 A65L Lightning differed from the touring models by fitting twin carburettors and a humped dualseat among its changes.

the use of straight spokes, and the non-brake side of the front hub was blanked off with a pressing. At the rear hub, this job was done by the sprocket, which was attached to the drum by four studs and nuts so that the rear wheel was quickly detachable.

Both front and rear brakes were of the single-leading-shoe type, and

through the middle of the rear fork pivot. A short lever-arm was splined to the right-hand end of this shaft and its end connected to the rear brake.

The original system used a cable to connect the lever to the rear brake, but this was later replaced by a two-stage rod design. With the latter, the short front rod ran to a

A Police version of the Lightning being tested by Bob Currie.

small link, pivoted from the frame, and picked up with the long rear rod, which ran to the brake cam lever.

Both wheels had 18 in. steel rims, the front being shod with a 3.25 in. ribbed tyre, and the back with a 3.50 in. universal type. Whitewall tyres were listed as an option, but found few takers. Well valanced mudguards kept the road dirt at bay, and the front was supported by a bridge plate and rear stay on each side. The rear mudguard was simply bolted to the frame and carried the rear number plate and its lamp.

The oil tank was rubber-mounted under the dualseat, while the tool-box was squeezed in behind it and within the right-side frame loop. This meant that it was barely large enough to accommodate the factory-packed tool roll, so once the owner had taken the tools out, there was little chance of getting them back. There was no possibility of adding extra tools to the kit within the toolbox.

The six-volt battery went in a carrier on the left-hand side of the machine next to the oil tank. The rectifier was tucked up in the corner of the subframe behind it, and the twin coils went in front of the oil tank with the drum-shaped air filter between them. The filter was one of the few parts that differed between the two models, and this was simply because they used different types of Monobloc carburettor.

Extensive side covers enclosed the area beneath the seat, and each was retained by a single quarter-turn fastener. The steel covers were each fitted with a 'flying wing' BSA badge and extended forward to enclose the carburettor and back to

fill the subframe loop.

The four gallon petrol tank was secured by a single fixing attached to the top tube, and this was concealed by a rubber plug. The tank itself was rubber-mounted and braced at the front by a bolted-on cross-member. It was fitted with twin taps, so it could be removed

Rider collecting a 1966 Lightning; riding gear, clothing and shop are all typical of the period.

The first road Spitfire was the 1966 MkII with twin Grand Prix carburettors and a fragile engine.

without draining, and was equipped with plain kneegrips and pear-shaped tank badges.

The exhaust system was simple, each of the two pipes being pushed into its respective port. At the other end went tubular silencers, one being mounted low down on each side. It was simple and efficient, with a mounting plate to attach the silencer to the pillion footrest mount-

ing loop, which was part of the subframe.

A deep guard was provided for the rear chain, but a further option was a chaincase giving full enclosure. This was in two parts and was attached to the rear fork leg by using the same fixing points as the stock guard.

The headlamp was mounted in a nacelle that carried the speedome-

For off-road use in 1966 in the USA, riders were offered this A50W Wasp with silencers but no lights.

This 1966 Spitfire Hornet was for more serious work, hence the open exhausts, but either off-road model could be made street-legal.

ter, ammeter and twin switches for lights and ignition. These controlled the electrical system with a combined horn button and dipswitch mounted on the handlebars. The other controls were conventional and included an air lever.

The finish of the new twins had the mudguards, side covers and petrol tank in colour, the last having chrome-plated side panels. The colour for the A50 was metallic green, while that for the A65 was Nutley blue, and the rest of the painted parts for both were in black. The wheel rims were chrome-plated, and the hubs and brake backplates were in silver sheen with polished rims. All-black versions of both models were available, and the A65 could be had in Flamboyant red as well.

Range extensions

The new twins sold well, although their podgy looks belied a loss of some 30 lb, compared with the older models. Somehow, the new ones lacked the lines and style of the past, seeming staid and lacking in spirit. They were bland rather than exciting.

Little was changed for 1963, other than the compression ratios, which went to 8.0:1 for the A50 and 7.5:1 for the A65. The ratio went up again for the A50 in 1964, when it reached 8.5:1, and both models could have 9.0:1 pistons fitted to order. Another change for 1964 was to the side covers, which were made more bulbous. This was to accommodate an extra battery on the A65 alone, for it was offered with 12 volt electrics as an option.

The two home-market models were joined by the Rocket A65R for 1964, and this had the 9.0:1 ratio pistons as standard, along with a hotter camshaft, folding kickstart and siamesed exhaust pipes leading to a single silencer low down on the right. The twin pipes remained available as an option, and the model could have a rev-counter, provided it was ordered and built in at the factory.

The rev-counter could not be simply added after purchase, as it

The 1967 Thunderbolt, little altered other than to a humped dualseat and finned rocker cover.

Firing up a 1966 Thunderbolt during a magazine road test. It took a good heave to start first thing in the morning!

was driven by a shaft that mated with the oil pump spindle. This shaft ran in a housing that provided the connection to the cable and was fitted to a different inner timing cover. A blanking plate could cover the hole if the drive was dispensed with and, in time, only the rev-counter type cover was listed.

Most of the rest of the A65R was common with the A65, so there was still only one carburettor, while the frame, wheels, brakes, seat, tank and side covers were the same. The forks were only altered in that they were fitted with gaiters and chrome-plated upper shrouds, which sup-

ported a separate headlamp shell in place of the nacelle. This shell still carried the ammeter and switches, but the speedometer was mounted on the top fork yoke, either by itself, or with the rev-counter on a common plate.

The finish of the A65R was in the same Flamboyant red that was an option for the touring model, but its mudguards were more sporting and were chrome-plated. The same range of touring options, such as legshields, handrail and safety bars, as were listed for the A50 and A65 were also available for the Rocket, but only that model could have ball-

The Lightning was essentially a twin-carburettor Thunderbolt and offered a higher level of performance than the tourer.

ended control levers.

In addition to the three home-market machines, there were four new derivatives for the USA. Only one, the A50 Cyclone Competition - or A50CC(US) - used the small engine, but this was in a tuned form with 10.5:1 compression ratio and twin 1-1/16 in. Monobloc carburet-tors, each with its own drum air filter. These were attached to a new cylinder head, which had splayed inlet ports. To accommodate the carburettors and filters, the side covers were reduced in size. Their material was changed to fibreglass, as this made it easier to achieve the desired alterations. Ignition was by

Timing side of the 1967 Spitfire in its MkIII form with Concentrics in place of the GPs.

Spitfire A65S MkIII for 1967 and here the subject of dreams.

energy transfer, and an open, waist-level exhaust pipe, with small protective legshield, went on each side.

The specification of the Cyclone was very much off-road, so there were no lights, but an undershield was fitted along with a small petrol tank and raised handlebars. The tyre sizes became 3.25 x 19 in. front and 4.00 x 18 in. rear, while both hubs were of the offset type, the rear being the famous quickly-detachable 'crinkle' hub. A centre stand was provided, while chrome-plated blade mudguards were fitted. There was neither speedometer nor rev-counter, but a full-length dualseat was fitted and the forks were gaitered.

The larger-capacity off-road machine was the Spitfire Hornet A65SH, which duplicated the Cyclone in most respects. It differed in having a rev-counter, twin 1-1/8 in. Monoblocs and either a 9.0 or 11.0:1 compression ratio. The front tyre section went up to 3.50 in., and the two gallon petrol tank was of fibre-glass with a transfer, and not as that of the Cyclone, which was of steel with chrome-plated side panels.

The remaining pair of twins were both built for the USA with high handlebars and were listed as the Thunderbolt A65T/R and the Lightning A65L/R. The first had the single-carburettor A65R engine unit and, in most respects, copied that model.

Dynamic picture of two BSA powered outfits battling for honours in very close company.

The Firebird Scrambler A65FS of 1968, which replaced the Hornet and was built as a street-scrambler with lights and silencers.

It kept to the same wheels and tyres, separate headlamp and gaitered forks, but could have a two or four gallon petrol tank. The front mudguard had more of a valance than that of the home-market Rocket, but continued to be chrome-plated, while round tank badges were fitted to the petrol tank.

The Lightning differed from the Thunderbolt in that it was fitted with the Hornet engine, with its twin carburettors, while the wheels had the offset hubs and 19 in. rims. Again,

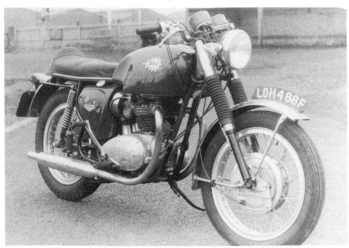

Final, MkIV, version of the Spitfire as built for 1968 with twin-leading-shoe front brake.

the petrol tank was of two or four gallon capacity and fitted with round badges.

All models had the option of a close-ratio gearbox, and a selection of gearbox and rear wheel sprockets was listed. Although the internal gear ratios were to be amended in 1967, the option remained available from then on.

Even more models appeared for 1965, the existing ones, except the Thunderbolt, continuing with no real change, other than to the A50, which was fitted with the 8 in. front brake. While the A65T/R was no more, as USA riders preferred the twin-carburettor Lightning, there were five new machines to amplify the range. Of these, only one was for the USA. This was the Cyclone A50C(US) road model which effectively, was the

Posed publicity shot of a 1968 Royal Star which had gained the humped dualseat by then.

Larger 1968 Thunderbolt with American style tank and bars, then fitted to all as standard.

Lightning, fitted with the Cyclone twin-carburettor engine running with 9.0:1 pistons. In other respects, it copied the larger model.

The other four machines that were new for 1965 were aimed at the home market and comprised sports and super-sports models in the two engine capacities. The smaller machines were the Cyclone A50C and Cyclone Clubman A50CC, while the larger were the Lightning A65L

For 1968 the Lightning was fitted with the twin-leading-shoe front brake which it needed to cope with its performance.

Posed Lightning, with its new full-width front hub, in nice environment in 1968.

and Lightning Clubman A65LC. All four had twin-carburettor engines, siamesed exhaust systems and wheels with offset hubs. Each of the sports pair was otherwise much as the Rocket model, but had a metallic gold finish for its petrol tank and side covers. The headlamp shell for each was chrome-plated, as were the sides of the petrol tank, and each machine was fitted with a rev-counter.

The Clubman versions were intended for production racing, so each had close-ratio gears, rear-sets, low handlebars and a humped du-

alseat. There was also a list of options, which included a fairing, five gallon petrol tank in light-alloy or fibreglass, alloy rims, clip-ons, twin-pipe exhaust systems, and the 190 mm front brake from the old Gold Star single.

This range of eleven models was really excessive and some, such as the various Cyclones, were seldom sold, as most customers went for the larger-capacity Lightning. So, for 1966, the range was reduced and simplified. Only six machines were left; two of 499 cc, and four of 654 cc, with two each for touring, sports

Royal Star for 1969, really little changed from the first A50 of seven years before.

and off-road, these last essentially export models.

All models had a number of common changes, and in the engine the most significant was to the drive-side main bearing, which became a lipped roller race. This was not the best of moves, for this type of race was never intended, nor was it able, to cope with axial loads. In theory, the shims held the end-float to an acceptable limit so that the loads were small. In practice, however, it was common for the crankshaft to pull one way or another, and at high speed its weight was too much for the shim pack.

The result of this problem could be traumatic, as the timing-side bush would move and cut off the oil supply, causing a seizure and leading to a rod through the crankcase. Thus, the fragile nature of the hottest twins was soon known, but in later years, a solution became available, although never from BSA. The answer was a combined axial and radial race to replace the timing-side bush, plus an oil feed into the end of the crankshaft, and it worked.

Inside the engine, there were generally bigger inlet valves than before and a timing notch in the flywheel, plus access to this at the front of the crankcase. On the outside, there was a balance pipe between the inlet tracts of the twin-carburettor models, and for the transmission, a three-spring clutch, which dictated a three-vane clutch shock absorber. The primary chaincase cover was altered to have one

The 1969
Thunderbolt which
was much as the
A50R, but in this
case has British
style handlebars
and tank.

access cap on the clutch centre-line, and another on its top shoulder for checking chain tension.

The frame was revised in detail, and the rear fork pivot no longer had the brake cross-shaft running in it, as the drum went on the left and its lever was connected directly to the pedal. The front forks gained two-way damping, and all models had them fitted with gaiters. All but one model had 8 in. front brakes in offset

Firebird Scrambler for 1969 with its lovely exhaust system curled along the left side.

hubs, the exception using the 190 mm brake with full-width hub. All models had a 7 in. rear brake and offset crinkle hub, with the rear wheel driving the speedometer.

The full chaincase option was no longer listed, and the nacelle had gone, to be replaced by a separate headlamp shell carrying the ammeter and light switch. The ignition switch went into the headstock on the left, and all models with a battery had a 12 volt electrical system.

ning A65L and the Spitfire MkII A65SS, the former much as the Thunderbolt, but with twin 1-5/32 in. carburettors and a humped dualseat.

The Spitfire was intended for production racing, so its engine had the compression ratio raised to 10.5:1, and it was fitted with twin Amal Grand Prix carburettors of the GP2 type and of 1-5/32 in. size. They were supplied by a 'Matchbox' type racing Amal float chamber, which was hung between the carburettors

Lightning for 1969, with exhaust balance pipe and twin windtone horns to herald its arrival.

Exceptions were the off-road models, which had energy-transfer ignition and no lights.

The touring models were the Royal Star A50R and Thunderbolt A65T, both of which had single-carburettor engines running on a 9.0:1 compression ratio. They had 3 gallon petrol tanks, with pear-shaped badges, and a flat dualseat. For the sports rider, there was the Light-

from a flexible mounting. It was fed by a five gallon fibreglass petrol tank, but a smaller tank, with a capacity of less than two gallons was optional. The standard tank had transfers for badges and knee-recesses in the sides. Equipment for the Spitfire included the 190 mm front brake along with alloy wheel rims, a racing dualseat and rev-counter as standard. It was very fast, but was soon

The A50R Royal Star in its final 1970 year when it still managed without the balance pipe but did have the better front brake.

Thunderbolt for 1970, little altered from the year before, but due for major changes.

found to be equally fragile.

For the off-road rider, there was the Wasp A50W and Hornet A65H, both much as the earlier A65H, but with variations in their cycle fitments. Both had highly-tuned engines with 10.5:1 compression ratios and twin carburettors. The Wasp was street-legal, as it had a speedometer and low-level exhaust pipes with silencers, but the Hornet retained the waist-level open pipes of the past. It was fitted with the humped dualseat, but the Wasp had the flat type, while both had fibreglass petrol tanks with capacities of under two gallons.

Tyres were to suit each machine's purpose, so all the road models had a 3.25 x 19 in. front, and all, except the Spitfire, a 3.50 x 19 in. rear. The Spitfire had a 4.00 x 18 in. tyre fitted to its rear wheel, and this size was

also used for the rear of the off-road pair, which had a 3.50 x 19 in. at the front.

Finishes were Flamboyant red for the petrol tank, side covers and mudguards of the Royal Star, and Flamboyant blue for the Thunderbolt, both having chrome-plated tank panels. The Lightning was as the Royal Star in red, except for chrome-plated mudguards, as was the Spitfire, except it lacked the plated tank panels. For off-road, the Wasp had Sapphire blue petrol tank and side covers, while the Hornet had these items in Mandarin red. Both had chrome-plated mudguards.

There were far fewer changes for 1967 when all six models continued, the Spitfire as the MkIII. For the engine, there was a new rocker box cover with fins, which was a direct replacement for the earlier type. A round cover appeared in the chaincase, in line with the crankshaft, so that the alternator rotor could be lit by a strobe light to check the ignition timing. Compression ratios were reduced a little to 10.0:1 for the Spitfire and Hornet, and the former had its carburettors changed to the cheaper Concentric type in the 932 size.

On the cycle side for 1967, all models had a dualseat with a hump, and all a 4.00 x 18 in. rear tyre. Some finishes changed, the Royal Star coloured items becoming Flamboyant blue, and those of the Thunderbolt black. The Lightning, Wasp and Hornet stayed as they were, and the Spitfire's colour became Royal red.

The make-up of the range was altered for 1968, as the Wasp was dropped and the Hornet became the Firebird Scrambler A65FS. The Spitfire reached its MkIV form, and the other models joined it in having Concentric carburettors. The A50 had a 626, the A65T a 928, and the A65L and A65FS a pair of 930s. All, except the scrambler, had 9.0:1 com-

The 1970 Lightning which, like the others, had few real changes, other than to the petrol tank.

Timing side of the 1970 Firebird Scrambler with its odd looks due to the absence of exhaust systems.

pression ratios, but the exception was back at 10.5:1.

The Spitfire lost the 190 mm front brake, joining the Lightning and Firebird in fitting a wheel with a full-width hub and 8in., twin-leading-shoe brake with air scoop for cooling. This had its two cam levers joined by a rod, the operating cable sweeping in from the rear to con-

Revised 1971 Thunderbolt with new frame of excessive seat height, and new forks, wheels and many details.

Thunderbolt 1971 detail showing the large top tube with filler cap, small side covers and air filter housing mouldings.

nect with the forward lever. To go with this hub, all three models changed to fork legs with split-ends that clamped around the wheel spindle. They also had rear suspension units with upper spring covers only.

For the export Firebird, the exhaust pipes were run to the silencers along the left side of the machine at waist level. It retained the rather small fibreglass petrol tank but, unlike the Hornet, the new model was more street oriented, having normal coil ignition, a battery and the same lighting equipment as the other models. For all, this included a toggle switch for the lights and a

red warning lamp, both set in the headlamp shell with the ammeter.

The 1968 finish included new die-cast alloy tank badges for three models, of which the Royal Star reverted to Flamboyant red, the Thunderbolt stayed in black, but gained chrome-plated mudguards, and the Lightning kept its Flamboyant red. The Spitfire remained in Royal red, and the Firebird Scrambler continued the red of the Hornet.

There were only four twins for 1969, as the Spitfire was replaced by the Rocket 3 triple. Those left had the alternator changed to an RM21, and both points and rotor covers

41

Lightning on road test in 1971, having its new cycle side design evaluated and given the practical test.

were amended to incorporate the company name. Exhaust balance pipes appeared close to the ports on the Thunderbolt and Lightning, and just in front of the silencers on the Firebird Scrambler, the compression ratio of which went down to 9.0:1.

All models gained fairing brackets on the frame headstock and shuttle damping in the front forks, but lost the rear spring unit covers. The revised forks had the split ends, and all models had the full-width front hub and twin-leading-shoe

brake. The brake linkage was revised so that the control cable could run down the fork leg, and to this end the front cam lever took a bellcrank form.

Twin windtone horns appeared on the Lightning, and an oil pressure switch was added to all engines. The road models had the option of two or four gallon petrol tanks, the former being supplied on the USA models, and the latter on the home-market ones. The Firebird continued with its small fibreglass tank and finish colour, as did the Thunderbolt and Lightning. The Royal Star's colour changed to Flamboyant blue and, alone, it continued with painted mudguards, although some had chrome-plated ones.

Little was altered for 1970, as the firm was heavily committed to planning major changes, so the existing four models ran on much as they were. The clutch lift mechanism was changed to a three-ball ramp type, but its operation was still unsatisfactory. Years later, the solution offered by one dealer was a replacement pressure plate with a needle thrust race. This helped the plates to lift squarely, kept the clutch pushrod centralised and made the mechanism much lighter in operation.

The Lightning adopted the Firebird tank shape for 1970, and the tanks for both models were made in steel rather than fibreglass. Finishes for the Royal Star and Thunderbolt were as those for 1969, in blue and black respectively, while the Lightning and Firebird continued in red with an option of blue.

This brought the range to November 1970 when there was a major relaunch by both BSA and Triumph as a joint exercise.

Final form

The new look, for both BSA and Triumph twins of 1971, came from the group design centre at Umberslade Hall. This had been set up to assist all the firms in the group, but had limited motorcycle knowledge and no real contact with the experts at Small Heath or Meriden. It was closed early in 1972, but by then, the damage had been done.

For 1971, the twin-cylinder range was reduced to three models, all with the 654 cc engine. Most parts were common to all three, and components such as the basic frame, forks, hubs, air cleaner box and many details were also common to Triumph twins. Both marques stood side-by-side at the extravagant launch, held in November 1970, with an array of other new or modified models beside them.

In reality, the group was already in deep financial trouble, which was made worse by major technical troubles with the 1971 ranges. As a result, some new models never reached production, the group did not tool-up for others, and the twins from both factories shared the problem of an excessive seat height.

The three remaining models were the A65T Thunderbolt with a single 928 carburettor, the A65L Lightning

Drive side of 1971 Firebird Scrambler with the new frame, old power unit, turn signals and matt black exhaust system.

Larger A70L
Lightning whose
engine has more
non-standard parts
than might be
expected. Stock
chassis.

with twin 930 instruments, and the A65FS Firebird Scrambler in trail format. The engine and gearbox unit was the same as in 1970, but the frame was completely new and carried the oil within its massive main tube. This single tube was formed as both top and seat tubes, with the oil filler cap at the bend under the dualseat nose. The base of the seat tube was filled by an oil filter which was, in effect, the bottom of the oil tank. Small pipes were inserted, as required for the feed and return pipes, while the rocker box continued to be lubricated by a take-off from the main return.

Duplex downtubes ran from the headstock, under the engine, and up to the dualseat loop and rear unit mountings. Cross tubes braced the frame, and the result was not too far removed from the 1970 frame. The new one continued to have fairing mountings on the headstock, and featured both centre and prop stands. An undershield was fitted to the Firebird Scrambler. The rear fork was supported by frame gusset-plates at each side, as before and also by a lug on the seat tube. It was controlled by a pair of spring-and-damper units, which lacked spring covers.

The frame was fitted with the group's new slimline design of telescopic fork, which had internal springs and was without gaiters to protect the stanchions. Cast-alloy fork legs were used, and each had its wheel spindle cap retained on four studs. Inside the forks, there was a new damping system, while taper-roller bearings were used for the head races. A steering damper remained available as an option.

Both wheels had the new conical hubs cast in light-alloy and spoked to steel rims. All three models had a 3.25 x 19 in. front tyre and a 4.00 x 18 in. rear one, while even the bolted-on rear wheel sprocket was common, the lower gearing of the A65FS being achieved by using a smaller gearbox sprocket.

An 8 in. brake with twin leading shoes went into the front hub, and its two, very short cam levers acted as the stops for the inner and outer cable ends. A click adjuster enabled each shoe to be adjusted, access to this being via a plugged hole in the conical hub. The brake shoes were mounted to a backplate that incorporated an air scoop plus twin exit holes for the cooling air. For the rear wheel, there was a conventional 7 in. single-leading-shoe brake, the backplate of which was anchored with a torque arm. Rear brake operation was by rod from a left-side pedal. The rear wheel was no longer quickly detachable, so a desirable facility was lost.

Even the off-road Firebird Scrambler was fitted with the stock, close-fitting, chrome-plated and unsprung front mudguard used by the other two twins. The mudguard had a single stay on each side, which was rubber mounted, with clamp plates and bushes, to the front fork leg. The rear mudguard was bolted directly to the frame and a combined support and handrail, which went behind the seat. This support carried the rear side reflectors, while the rear turn signals, with which even the Firebird Scrambler was fitted,were screwed into the sides of the rear light bracket.

Lucas switches and buttons, fitted into the handlebar control lever mounting blocks, provided the elec-

Final, 1972 Thunderbolt which was little altered from the year before.

trical functions, but with little to identify them. They also lacked the ergonomics to which riders were becoming accustomed. All models had the same handlebar bend, but there were minor variations in the controls fitted to it.

A shallow, pan-shaped, headlamp shell was used and held by a pair of bent wires, each of which was rubber-mounted to the fork crowns. The main light switch went in the top of

tors, so there were sets of mouldings with either single or twin hoses to connect to the carburettor intakes. The outer mouldings had dummy louvres formed in them for style, but the whole design involved excessive tooling costs for what it produced.

On the exhaust side, the two road models had pipes that were joined close to the ports by a balance pipe. Each exhaust pipe swept down to a

The BSA T65 Thunderbolt of 1973, which was a Triumph TR6 from that year, but fitted with earlier forks and front wheel.

the shell, and a trio of warning lights in its rear surface. The front turn-signal stalks were used to hold the shell to its wire supports. The ignition switch was in the right-hand side panel which, together with the matching one on the left, fitted in behind the air filter housings to fill the subframe corners.

The air filter housing assembly comprised four mouldings that went together to form two housings, one on each side. These were joined in the middle of the machine, and all models had two filter elements in the housings. The detail parts varied to suit the number of carburet-

megaphone silencer mounted low down on the side of the machine. For the Firebird Scrambler, both pipes curled round to the left-hand side of the machine, where they ran back at waist level. They were joined by a balance connector just in front of the twin silencers, which sat one above the other. The complete exhaust system was finished in matt black and fitted with a chrome-plated wire grille to protect the rider and passenger from burns.

All three models had the same petrol tank for export, and this carried 'winged' BSA badges held by small screws. For the home-market

Tony Smith with his BSA twin which was very successful in production racing.

road models, there were larger tanks with transfers. A speedometer was provided for all three models, but the Thunderbolt managed without the rev-counter supplied for the other two. The instrument heads were carried in rubber cups, which were fitted into mounting plates held by the fork top nuts.

The finish of all three was similar, the frame being in a Dove grey, which showed up the dirt far too easily. The mudguards, headlamp shell and wheel rims were chrome-plated, while the side covers, air filter boxes and petrol tank were painted. The tank was in a single colour for the home market, but the USA machines had this combined with a white lower section. The colours were Sterling Moss green for the Thunderbolt, and bronze for the other two.

There was little real change for 1972, as the firm was in far too much financial trouble by then. Only the

Thunderbolt and Lightning remained, but they were joined by a larger version of the latter, the A70L model. This was built solely for the USA to form the basis of a dirt-track machine. To meet the ruling that machines had to be based on road models, BSA had to build at least 200 of them.

The extra capacity came from extending the stroke to 85 mm, which resulted in 751 cc, while the compression ratio went up to 9.5:1, but the twin 930 Amal carburettors remained. In addition to the crankshaft, the engine had a number of other parts that differed from those in the 650 unit, including the crankcase, pistons, rods and flywheel, as well as some minor details. A small number of these engines remained in Britain and some did finish up in complete machines. The rest went to America where they were also known as the Lightning 75.

The A70L was finished as the A65L

Jim Rice with the flat-track twin fitted here with disc brakes to both wheels.

in Firebird red, while the A65T was in Etruscan bronze for 1972. All models reverted to the traditional black for the frame, while the front brake backplate was finished in matt black.

This proved to be the last year for the BSA unit twins, as the company's financial problems grew worse. The issues became complex, but the result for BSA was simply that the firm closed, and in later years, the factory was demolished.

It was not the end of the BSA name which, in time, returned on a variety of small machines, but the only twin of relevance here was the T65 Thunderbolt. This appeared for 1973, but the only link with BSA

was the name on the tank and side panels. In all other respects, the machine was a Triumph TR6 of that year, but fitted with older, gaitered front forks and the full-width hub with twin-leading-shoe brake of the late 1960s.

While BSA has now long gone in its Small Heath form, the A50 and A65 series of twins lives on and has been one of the more popular in the classic revival of the 1980s. With most parts available, and a good background of information and data to be had, they are among the easier machines to restore and offer good performance on the road and fine motorcycling.

Competition unit twins

BSA twins were normally over-shadowed by their singles for competition work, but there were exceptions, especially for sidecar road racing. The unit twins were also used solo, both at home and abroad, but rarely off-road. One exception to this was the 1962 ISDT, where John Harris rode a 499 cc twin, with suitable fixtures and fittings, as a member of the British Trophy team, and won a gold medal.

Sidecar racing in the United Kingdom was dominated by Chris Vincent in the 1960s, first with a pre-unit BSA twin and then, from 1964, with unit engines. This encouraged other drivers to use the same power unit, so the BSA twins came to dominate sidecar racing in Britain, several of the leading men, as well as Vincent, being employed by BSA.

The twins were not so dominant in solo production racing, although Bob Heath and Tony Smith, both BSA employees, were successful against the hoards of Triumph Bonnevilles in that class. More publicised was Mike Hailwood's win in the 1965 Hutchinson 100 production race on an A65L. In pouring rain, he headed Phil Read and Percy Tait on Triumphs at the line, on a day when he also won races using single- and four-cylinder machines.

In 1966 and 1967, BSA ran a team

Peter Brown during the 1970 750 cc sidecar TT in which his BSA outfit took second place.

Problems for the Tony Smith Spitfire, with its fairing in two pieces and not to the liking of the scrutineer.

of twins at Daytona, but without any success. This American exercise led to flat-track twins during this period, these being set up specifically to suit this specialised form of motorcycle sport. In time, the larger BSA and Triumph triples took over for the Daytona event, but the lighter twins continued in flat-track events.

At home, the twins and triples proved to be evenly matched in production racing at first, but the edge was with the triples, once riders became used to the weight and power. For sidecar racing, the low and compact twin remained in fa-

vour well into the 1970s when the two-strokes finally took over.

The unit-twin BSA suited the sidecars, thanks to its smooth power delivery. Most proved quite reliable on the circuits, even when racing every weekend, but this was no doubt partly because some were raced by factory personnel who benefited from factory knowledge. This ensured that any doubtful areas were attended to before trouble arose but, sadly, the factory seemed disinclined to use this information to improve the production machines.

BSA Unit Twins Specifications

All models have two cylinders, overhead valves, alternator, four-speed gearbox and a frame with telescopic front and pivoted-fork rear suspension.

Model	A50	A50CC(US)	A50C(US)	A50C(UK)	A50CC(UK)	A65
years	1962-65	1964-65	1965	1965	1965	1962-65
bore mm	65.5	65.5	65.5	65.5	65.5	75
stroke mm	74	74	74	74	74	74
capacity cc	499	499	499	499	499	654
comp. ratio	7.25[1]	10.5	9.0	9.0	9.0	7.25[2]
carb type	376	376 (2)	376 (2)	376 (2)	376 (2)	389
carb size	1	1-1/16	1-1/16	1-1/16	1-1/16	1-1/8
ignition by	coil	ET	coil	coil	coil	coil
electrics volts	6	-	6	6	6	6[3]
top gear	5.12	5.18	5.18	5.12	5.12	4.35
petrol - gall	4	2	2	4	4 or 5	4
front tyre	3.25x18	3.25x19	3.25x19	3.25x19	3.25x19	3.25x18
rear tyre	3.50x18	4.00x18	4.00x18	3.50x19	3.50x19	3.50x18
front brake dia	7[4]	8	8	8	8 or 190mm	8
rear brake dia	7	7	7	7	7	7
wheelbase in.	54.1	56	56	56	56	54.1

[1] - 1963-8.0, 1964-8.5   [2] - 1963-7.5
[3] - 1964-12 volt option   [4] - 1965-8

BSA Unit Twins Specifications

Model	A65R	A65T/R	A65L/R	A65SH	A65L	A65LC
years	1964-65	1964	1964-65	1964-65	1965	1965
bore mm	75	75	75	75	75	75
stroke mm	74	74	74	74	74	74
capacity cc	654	654	654	654	654	654
comp. ratio	9.0	9.0	9.0	9 or 11	9.0	9.0
carb type	389	389	389 (2)	389 (2)	389 (2)	389 (2)
carb size	1-1/8	1-1/8	1-1/8	1-1/8	1-1/8	1-1/8
ignition by	coil	coil	coil	ET	coil	coil
electrics volts	6	6	6	-	6	6
top gear	4.35	4.58	4.58	4.14	4.58	4.58
petrol - gall	4	2 or 4	2 or 4	2	4	4 or 5
front tyre	3.25x18	3.25x18	3.25x19	3.50x19	3.25x19	3.25x19
rear tyre	3.50x18	3.50x18	3.50x19	4.00x18	3.50x19	3.50x19
front brake dia	8	8	8	8	8	8 or 190mm
rear brake dia	7	7	7	7	7	7
wheelbase in.	54.1	54.1	56	56	56	56

BSA Unit Twins Specifications

Model	A50R	A50W	A65T	A65L	A65S	A65H
years	1966-70	1966-67	1966-70	1966-70	1966-68	1966-67
bore mm	65.5	65.5	75	75	75	75
stroke mm	74	74	74	74	74	74
capacity cc	499	499	654	654	654	654
comp. ratio	9.0	10.5	9.0	9.0	10.5[1]	10.5[1]
carb type	376[2]	389 (2)	389[3]	389 (2)[4]	GP(2)[5]	389(2)
carb size	1[6]	1-1/8	1-1/8[7]	1-5/32[8]	1-5/32[9]	1-5/32
ignition by	coil	ET	coil	coil	coil	ET
electrics volts	12	-	12	12	12	-
top gear	5.41	5.41	4.87	4.87	4.64[10]	4.87[11]
petrol - gall	3.5[12]	1.9	3.5[13]	3.5[13]	1.9 or 5[14]	1.9
front tyre	3.25x19	3.50x19	3.25x19	3.25x19	3.25x19	3.50x19
rear tyre	3.50x19[15]	4.00x18	3.50x19[15]	3.50x19[15]	4.00x18	4.00x18
front brake dia	8	8	8	8	190mm[16]	8
rear brake dia	7	7	7	7	7	7
wheelbase in.	56	56	56	56	56	56

[1] - 1967-10.0, 1968-9.0   [2] - 1968-626   [3] - 1968-928
[4] - 1968-930   [5] - 1967-932   [6] - 1968-26mm
[7] - 1968-28mm   [8] - 1968-30mm   [9] - 1967-32mm
[10] - 1967-4.87   [11] - 1967-5.73
[12] - 1967-2.75, 1969-2.75 or 4   [13] - 1967-2.75, 1968-2.75 or 4   [14] - 1967-1.9 or 4
[15] - 1967-4.00x18   [16] - 1968-8

BSA Unit Twins Specifications

Model	A65FS	A65T	A65L	A65FS	A70L	T65
years	1968-70	1971-72	1971-72	1971	1972	1973
bore mm	75	75	75	75	75	71
stroke mm	74	74	74	74	85	82
capacity cc	654	654	654	654	751	649
comp. ratio	10.5[1]	9.0	9.0	9.0	9.5	9.0
carb type	930 (2)	928	930(2)	930 (2)	930 (2)	930
carb size	30mm	28mm	30mm	30mm	30mm	30mm
ignition by	coil	coil	coil	coil	coil	coil
electrics volts	12	12	12	12	12	12
top gear	4.87	4.87	4.87	5.41	4.64	4.95
petrol - gall	1.9[2]	2.5 or 4	2.5 or 4	2.5	2.5 or 4	4
front tyre	3.50x19	3.25x19	3.25x19	3.25x19	3.25x19	3.25x19
rear tyre	4.00x18	4.00x18	4.00x18	4.00x18	4.00x18	4.00x18
front brake dia	8	8	8	8	8	8
rear brake dia	7	7	7	7	7	7
wheelbase in.	56	56	56	56	56	-

[1] - 1968-9.0   [2] - 1969-2.5, 1970-2.75 or 3.25